50 Beyond Breakfast Pancake Recipes for Home

By: Kelly Johnson

Table of Contents

- Classic Buttermilk Pancakes
- Blueberry Lemon Pancakes
- Banana Walnut Pancakes
- Chocolate Chip Pancakes
- Cinnamon Roll Pancakes
- Pumpkin Spice Pancakes
- Apple Cinnamon Pancakes
- Coconut Flour Pancakes
- Oatmeal Pancakes
- Peanut Butter Banana Pancakes
- Strawberry Shortcake Pancakes
- Matcha Green Tea Pancakes
- Almond Flour Pancakes
- Ricotta Pancakes
- Nutella Stuffed Pancakes
- Sweet Potato Pancakes
- Carrot Cake Pancakes
- Orange Zest Pancakes
- Chia Seed Pancakes
- Cornmeal Pancakes
- Sourdough Pancakes
- Raspberry Almond Pancakes
- Chocolate Avocado Pancakes
- Gingerbread Pancakes
- Maple Pecan Pancakes
- Zucchini Pancakes
- Tahini Banana Pancakes
- Lemon Poppy Seed Pancakes
- Blackberry Coconut Pancakes
- Peanut Butter Cup Pancakes
- Tiramisu Pancakes
- Dulce de Leche Pancakes
- Espresso Pancakes
- Key Lime Pancakes
- Vegan Blueberry Pancakes

- Savory Spinach and Feta Pancakes
- Strawberry Basil Pancakes
- Funfetti Pancakes
- Honey Almond Pancakes
- Matcha Coconut Pancakes
- Chocolate Peanut Butter Pancakes
- Maple Bacon Pancakes
- Muesli Pancakes
- Raspberry Coconut Pancakes
- Pistachio Pancakes
- Thai Coconut Pancakes
- Pear Ginger Pancakes
- Tofu Pancakes
- Cherry Almond Pancakes
- Mocha Pancakes

Classic Buttermilk Pancakes

Ingredients:

- 1 cup all-purpose flour
- 2 tbsp sugar
- 1 tsp baking powder
- 1/2 tsp baking soda
- 1/4 tsp salt
- 1 cup buttermilk
- 1 large egg
- 2 tbsp melted butter

Instructions:

1. In a bowl, whisk together flour, sugar, baking powder, baking soda, and salt.
2. In another bowl, mix buttermilk, egg, and melted butter.
3. Combine wet and dry ingredients, stirring until just combined.
4. Heat a skillet over medium heat, pour batter, and cook until bubbles form. Flip and cook until golden.

Blueberry Lemon Pancakes

Ingredients:

- 1 cup all-purpose flour
- 1 tbsp sugar
- 1 tsp baking powder
- 1/2 tsp baking soda
- 1/4 tsp salt
- 1 cup buttermilk
- 1 large egg
- 1/2 cup blueberries
- Zest of 1 lemon

Instructions:

1. In a bowl, whisk flour, sugar, baking powder, baking soda, and salt.
2. In another bowl, mix buttermilk, egg, and lemon zest.
3. Combine wet and dry ingredients, then gently fold in blueberries.
4. Cook on a heated skillet until bubbles appear, then flip and cook until golden.

Banana Walnut Pancakes

Ingredients:

- 1 cup all-purpose flour
- 2 tbsp sugar
- 1 tsp baking powder
- 1/2 tsp baking soda
- 1/4 tsp salt
- 1 cup buttermilk
- 1 large egg
- 1 ripe banana, mashed
- 1/2 cup chopped walnuts

Instructions:

1. In a bowl, whisk flour, sugar, baking powder, baking soda, and salt.
2. In another bowl, combine buttermilk, egg, and mashed banana.
3. Mix wet and dry ingredients, then fold in walnuts.
4. Cook on a skillet until bubbles form, then flip and cook until golden.

Chocolate Chip Pancakes

Ingredients:

- 1 cup all-purpose flour
- 2 tbsp sugar
- 1 tsp baking powder
- 1/2 tsp baking soda
- 1/4 tsp salt
- 1 cup buttermilk
- 1 large egg
- 1/2 cup chocolate chips

Instructions:

1. Whisk together flour, sugar, baking powder, baking soda, and salt.
2. In another bowl, mix buttermilk and egg.
3. Combine wet and dry ingredients, then fold in chocolate chips.
4. Cook on a skillet until bubbles appear, flip, and cook until golden.

Cinnamon Roll Pancakes

Ingredients:

- 1 cup all-purpose flour
- 2 tbsp sugar
- 1 tsp baking powder
- 1/2 tsp baking soda
- 1/4 tsp salt
- 1 cup buttermilk
- 1 large egg
- 2 tbsp cinnamon sugar (1 tbsp cinnamon + 1 tbsp sugar)
- Cream cheese frosting (for drizzling)

Instructions:

1. Whisk flour, sugar, baking powder, baking soda, and salt.
2. In another bowl, mix buttermilk and egg.
3. Combine wet and dry ingredients, then swirl in cinnamon sugar.
4. Cook on a skillet, flipping once golden; drizzle with cream cheese frosting.

Pumpkin Spice Pancakes

Ingredients:

- 1 cup all-purpose flour
- 2 tbsp sugar
- 1 tsp baking powder
- 1/2 tsp baking soda
- 1/4 tsp salt
- 1 cup buttermilk
- 1 large egg
- 1/2 cup pumpkin puree
- 1 tsp pumpkin pie spice

Instructions:

1. In a bowl, whisk flour, sugar, baking powder, baking soda, salt, and pumpkin pie spice.
2. In another bowl, mix buttermilk, egg, and pumpkin puree.
3. Combine wet and dry ingredients.
4. Cook on a skillet until bubbles appear, then flip and cook until golden.

Apple Cinnamon Pancakes

Ingredients:

- 1 cup all-purpose flour
- 2 tbsp sugar
- 1 tsp baking powder
- 1/2 tsp baking soda
- 1/4 tsp salt
- 1 cup buttermilk
- 1 large egg
- 1 apple, grated
- 1 tsp cinnamon

Instructions:

1. Whisk together flour, sugar, baking powder, baking soda, salt, and cinnamon.
2. In another bowl, mix buttermilk and egg.
3. Combine wet and dry ingredients, then fold in grated apple.
4. Cook on a skillet until bubbles form, flip, and cook until golden.

Coconut Flour Pancakes

Ingredients:

- 1/2 cup coconut flour
- 4 large eggs
- 1/2 cup milk (dairy or non-dairy)
- 2 tbsp honey or maple syrup
- 1/4 tsp salt
- 1/2 tsp baking powder

Instructions:

1. In a bowl, whisk coconut flour, salt, and baking powder.
2. In another bowl, mix eggs, milk, and honey.
3. Combine wet and dry ingredients until smooth.
4. Cook on a skillet until golden, flipping once.

Enjoy these delightful pancake recipes!

Oatmeal Pancakes

Ingredients:

- 1 cup rolled oats
- 1 cup milk (dairy or non-dairy)
- 1/2 cup all-purpose flour
- 1 tbsp sugar
- 1 tsp baking powder
- 1/2 tsp baking soda
- 1/4 tsp salt
- 1 large egg
- 1 tsp vanilla extract

Instructions:

1. In a bowl, soak oats in milk for about 10 minutes.
2. In another bowl, mix flour, sugar, baking powder, baking soda, and salt.
3. Combine the soaked oats with the dry ingredients, then add egg and vanilla.
4. Cook on a heated skillet until bubbles form, then flip and cook until golden.

Peanut Butter Banana Pancakes

Ingredients:

- 1 cup all-purpose flour
- 1 tbsp sugar
- 1 tsp baking powder
- 1/2 tsp baking soda
- 1/4 tsp salt
- 1 cup milk
- 1 ripe banana, mashed
- 1/4 cup peanut butter
- 1 tsp vanilla extract

Instructions:

1. In a bowl, whisk flour, sugar, baking powder, baking soda, and salt.
2. In another bowl, mix milk, banana, peanut butter, and vanilla.
3. Combine wet and dry ingredients until just mixed.
4. Cook on a skillet until bubbles appear, flip, and cook until golden.

Strawberry Shortcake Pancakes

Ingredients:

- 1 cup all-purpose flour
- 2 tbsp sugar
- 1 tsp baking powder
- 1/2 tsp baking soda
- 1/4 tsp salt
- 1 cup buttermilk
- 1 large egg
- 1 cup strawberries, sliced
- Whipped cream (for serving)

Instructions:

1. In a bowl, whisk flour, sugar, baking powder, baking soda, and salt.
2. In another bowl, mix buttermilk and egg.
3. Combine wet and dry ingredients, gently folding in strawberries.
4. Cook on a skillet until golden, then serve topped with whipped cream and extra strawberries.

Matcha Green Tea Pancakes

Ingredients:

- 1 cup all-purpose flour
- 2 tbsp sugar
- 1 tsp baking powder
- 1/2 tsp baking soda
- 1/4 tsp salt
- 1 tbsp matcha powder
- 1 cup milk
- 1 large egg
- 1 tsp vanilla extract

Instructions:

1. In a bowl, whisk flour, sugar, baking powder, baking soda, salt, and matcha.
2. In another bowl, mix milk, egg, and vanilla.
3. Combine wet and dry ingredients until just mixed.
4. Cook on a skillet until bubbles form, then flip and cook until golden.

Almond Flour Pancakes

Ingredients:

- 1 cup almond flour
- 2 large eggs
- 1/4 cup milk (dairy or non-dairy)
- 1 tbsp honey or maple syrup
- 1/2 tsp baking powder
- 1/4 tsp salt

Instructions:

1. In a bowl, mix almond flour, baking powder, and salt.
2. In another bowl, whisk eggs, milk, and honey.
3. Combine wet and dry ingredients until smooth.
4. Cook on a skillet until golden, flipping once.

Ricotta Pancakes

Ingredients:

- 1 cup ricotta cheese
- 2 large eggs
- 1/2 cup all-purpose flour
- 1 tbsp sugar
- 1 tsp baking powder
- 1/4 tsp salt
- Zest of 1 lemon (optional)

Instructions:

1. In a bowl, whisk together ricotta, eggs, and lemon zest.
2. In another bowl, mix flour, sugar, baking powder, and salt.
3. Combine wet and dry ingredients until just mixed.
4. Cook on a skillet until golden, flipping once.

Nutella Stuffed Pancakes

Ingredients:

- 1 cup all-purpose flour
- 2 tbsp sugar
- 1 tsp baking powder
- 1/2 tsp baking soda
- 1/4 tsp salt
- 1 cup milk
- 1 large egg
- Nutella (for stuffing)

Instructions:

1. In a bowl, whisk flour, sugar, baking powder, baking soda, and salt.
2. In another bowl, mix milk and egg.
3. Combine wet and dry ingredients until just mixed.
4. Pour batter on a skillet, add a spoonful of Nutella on top, then cover with more batter. Cook until golden, flipping once.

Sweet Potato Pancakes

Ingredients:

- 1 cup mashed sweet potatoes
- 1 cup all-purpose flour
- 1 tbsp sugar
- 1 tsp baking powder
- 1/2 tsp baking soda
- 1/4 tsp salt
- 1 cup milk
- 1 large egg
- 1 tsp cinnamon

Instructions:

1. In a bowl, mix mashed sweet potatoes, flour, sugar, baking powder, baking soda, salt, and cinnamon.
2. In another bowl, whisk milk and egg, then combine with the dry mixture.
3. Cook on a skillet until bubbles form, then flip and cook until golden.

Enjoy these delicious pancake variations!

Carrot Cake Pancakes

Ingredients:

- 1 cup all-purpose flour
- 1 tbsp sugar
- 1 tsp baking powder
- 1/2 tsp baking soda
- 1/4 tsp salt
- 1 tsp cinnamon
- 1/2 cup grated carrots
- 1 cup buttermilk
- 1 large egg
- 1/4 cup walnuts, chopped (optional)

Instructions:

1. In a bowl, whisk flour, sugar, baking powder, baking soda, salt, and cinnamon.
2. In another bowl, mix buttermilk, egg, and grated carrots.
3. Combine wet and dry ingredients, folding in walnuts if using.
4. Cook on a skillet until bubbles form, then flip and cook until golden.

Orange Zest Pancakes

Ingredients:

- 1 cup all-purpose flour
- 2 tbsp sugar
- 1 tsp baking powder
- 1/2 tsp baking soda
- 1/4 tsp salt
- 1 cup milk
- 1 large egg
- Zest of 1 orange
- 1 tsp vanilla extract

Instructions:

1. In a bowl, whisk flour, sugar, baking powder, baking soda, and salt.
2. In another bowl, mix milk, egg, orange zest, and vanilla.
3. Combine wet and dry ingredients until just mixed.
4. Cook on a skillet until golden, flipping once.

Chia Seed Pancakes

Ingredients:

- 1 cup all-purpose flour
- 1 tbsp sugar
- 1 tsp baking powder
- 1/2 tsp baking soda
- 1/4 tsp salt
- 1 tbsp chia seeds
- 1 cup milk
- 1 large egg
- 1 tsp vanilla extract

Instructions:

1. In a bowl, whisk flour, sugar, baking powder, baking soda, salt, and chia seeds.
2. In another bowl, mix milk, egg, and vanilla.
3. Combine wet and dry ingredients until just mixed.
4. Cook on a skillet until bubbles form, then flip and cook until golden.

Cornmeal Pancakes

Ingredients:

- 1 cup cornmeal
- 1/2 cup all-purpose flour
- 2 tbsp sugar
- 1 tsp baking powder
- 1/2 tsp baking soda
- 1/4 tsp salt
- 1 cup milk
- 1 large egg
- 2 tbsp melted butter

Instructions:

1. In a bowl, whisk cornmeal, flour, sugar, baking powder, baking soda, and salt.
2. In another bowl, mix milk, egg, and melted butter.
3. Combine wet and dry ingredients until just mixed.
4. Cook on a skillet until golden, flipping once.

Sourdough Pancakes

Ingredients:

- 1 cup sourdough starter
- 1 cup milk
- 1 large egg
- 1 tbsp sugar
- 1 tsp baking powder
- 1/2 tsp baking soda
- 1/4 tsp salt
- 1 cup all-purpose flour

Instructions:

1. In a bowl, mix sourdough starter, milk, egg, and sugar.
2. In another bowl, whisk flour, baking powder, baking soda, and salt.
3. Combine wet and dry ingredients until just mixed.
4. Cook on a skillet until bubbles form, then flip and cook until golden.

Raspberry Almond Pancakes

Ingredients:

- 1 cup all-purpose flour
- 2 tbsp sugar
- 1 tsp baking powder
- 1/2 tsp baking soda
- 1/4 tsp salt
- 1 cup milk
- 1 large egg
- 1/2 cup raspberries
- 1/4 cup sliced almonds

Instructions:

1. In a bowl, whisk flour, sugar, baking powder, baking soda, and salt.
2. In another bowl, mix milk and egg.
3. Combine wet and dry ingredients, gently folding in raspberries and almonds.
4. Cook on a skillet until bubbles appear, then flip and cook until golden.

Chocolate Avocado Pancakes

Ingredients:

- 1 cup all-purpose flour
- 2 tbsp cocoa powder
- 1 tbsp sugar
- 1 tsp baking powder
- 1/2 tsp baking soda
- 1/4 tsp salt
- 1 ripe avocado, mashed
- 1 cup milk
- 1 large egg

Instructions:

1. In a bowl, whisk flour, cocoa powder, sugar, baking powder, baking soda, and salt.
2. In another bowl, mix mashed avocado, milk, and egg until smooth.
3. Combine wet and dry ingredients until just mixed.
4. Cook on a skillet until bubbles form, then flip and cook until golden.

Gingerbread Pancakes

Ingredients:

- 1 cup all-purpose flour
- 2 tbsp brown sugar
- 1 tsp baking powder
- 1/2 tsp baking soda
- 1/4 tsp salt
- 1 tsp ground ginger
- 1 tsp cinnamon
- 1/4 tsp nutmeg
- 1 cup milk
- 1 large egg
- 1/4 cup molasses

Instructions:

1. In a bowl, whisk flour, brown sugar, baking powder, baking soda, salt, ginger, cinnamon, and nutmeg.
2. In another bowl, mix milk, egg, and molasses.
3. Combine wet and dry ingredients until just mixed.
4. Cook on a skillet until golden, flipping once.

Enjoy these delicious pancake recipes!

Maple Pecan Pancakes

Ingredients:
1 cup all-purpose flour
2 tbsp sugar
1 tsp baking powder
1/2 tsp baking soda
1/4 tsp salt
1 cup milk
1 large egg
1/2 cup chopped pecans
1/4 cup maple syrup

Instructions:
In a bowl, whisk flour, sugar, baking powder, baking soda, and salt. In another bowl, mix milk, egg, and maple syrup. Combine wet and dry ingredients, folding in pecans. Cook on a skillet until golden, flipping once.

Zucchini Pancakes

Ingredients:
1 cup all-purpose flour
1 tbsp sugar
1 tsp baking powder
1/2 tsp baking soda
1/4 tsp salt
1 cup grated zucchini
1 cup milk
1 large egg
1 tsp garlic powder (optional)

Instructions:
In a bowl, whisk flour, sugar, baking powder, baking soda, salt, and garlic powder if using. In another bowl, mix grated zucchini, milk, and egg. Combine wet and dry ingredients. Cook on a skillet until golden, flipping once.

Tahini Banana Pancakes

Ingredients:
1 cup all-purpose flour
1 tbsp sugar
1 tsp baking powder
1/2 tsp baking soda
1/4 tsp salt
1 ripe banana, mashed
1/4 cup tahini
1 cup milk
1 large egg

Instructions:
In a bowl, whisk flour, sugar, baking powder, baking soda, and salt. In another bowl, mix mashed banana, tahini, milk, and egg. Combine wet and dry ingredients until just mixed. Cook on a skillet until bubbles form, then flip and cook until golden.

Lemon Poppy Seed Pancakes

Ingredients:
1 cup all-purpose flour
2 tbsp sugar
1 tsp baking powder
1/2 tsp baking soda
1/4 tsp salt
1 cup milk
1 large egg
Zest of 1 lemon
1 tbsp poppy seeds

Instructions:
In a bowl, whisk flour, sugar, baking powder, baking soda, and salt. In another bowl, mix milk, egg, lemon zest, and poppy seeds. Combine wet and dry ingredients. Cook on a skillet until golden, flipping once.

Blackberry Coconut Pancakes

Ingredients:
1 cup all-purpose flour
2 tbsp sugar
1 tsp baking powder
1/2 tsp baking soda
1/4 tsp salt
1 cup coconut milk
1 large egg
1/2 cup blackberries
1/4 cup shredded coconut

Instructions:
In a bowl, whisk flour, sugar, baking powder, baking soda, and salt. In another bowl, mix coconut milk and egg. Combine wet and dry ingredients, gently folding in blackberries and coconut. Cook on a skillet until golden, flipping once.

Peanut Butter Cup Pancakes

Ingredients:
1 cup all-purpose flour
2 tbsp cocoa powder
1 tbsp sugar
1 tsp baking powder
1/2 tsp baking soda
1/4 tsp salt
1 cup milk
1 large egg
1/4 cup peanut butter
1/4 cup chocolate chips

Instructions:
In a bowl, whisk flour, cocoa powder, sugar, baking powder, baking soda, and salt. In another bowl, mix milk, egg, and peanut butter until smooth. Combine wet and dry ingredients, folding in chocolate chips. Cook on a skillet until bubbles form, then flip and cook until golden.

Tiramisu Pancakes

Ingredients:
1 cup all-purpose flour
2 tbsp sugar
1 tsp baking powder
1/2 tsp baking soda
1/4 tsp salt
1 cup milk
1 large egg
2 tbsp coffee, cooled
1/4 cup mascarpone cheese
Cocoa powder (for dusting)

Instructions:
In a bowl, whisk flour, sugar, baking powder, baking soda, and salt. In another bowl, mix milk, egg, and coffee. Combine wet and dry ingredients. Cook on a skillet until golden, flipping once. Serve dusted with cocoa and a dollop of mascarpone.

Dulce de Leche Pancakes

Ingredients:
1 cup all-purpose flour
2 tbsp sugar
1 tsp baking powder
1/2 tsp baking soda
1/4 tsp salt
1 cup milk
1 large egg
1/4 cup dulce de leche

Instructions:
In a bowl, whisk flour, sugar, baking powder, baking soda, and salt. In another bowl, mix milk, egg, and dulce de leche until smooth. Combine wet and dry ingredients until just mixed. Cook on a skillet until golden, flipping once.

Enjoy these delightful pancake recipes!

Espresso Pancakes

Ingredients:
1 cup all-purpose flour
2 tbsp sugar
1 tsp baking powder
1/2 tsp baking soda
1/4 tsp salt
1 cup milk
1 large egg
2 tbsp brewed espresso
1/4 cup chocolate chips (optional)

Instructions:
In a bowl, whisk flour, sugar, baking powder, baking soda, and salt. In another bowl, mix milk, egg, and espresso. Combine wet and dry ingredients, folding in chocolate chips if desired. Cook on a skillet until golden, flipping once.

Key Lime Pancakes

Ingredients:
1 cup all-purpose flour
2 tbsp sugar
1 tsp baking powder
1/2 tsp baking soda
1/4 tsp salt
1 cup milk
1 large egg
Zest of 1 lime
1/4 cup key lime juice

Instructions:
In a bowl, whisk flour, sugar, baking powder, baking soda, and salt. In another bowl, mix milk, egg, lime zest, and juice. Combine wet and dry ingredients. Cook on a skillet until golden, flipping once.

Vegan Blueberry Pancakes

Ingredients:
1 cup all-purpose flour
2 tbsp sugar
1 tsp baking powder
1/2 tsp baking soda
1/4 tsp salt
1 cup almond milk (or other plant milk)
1 tbsp ground flaxseed mixed with 2.5 tbsp water (flax egg)
1/2 cup blueberries

Instructions:
In a bowl, whisk flour, sugar, baking powder, baking soda, and salt. In another bowl, mix almond milk and flax egg. Combine wet and dry ingredients, gently folding in blueberries. Cook on a skillet until golden, flipping once.

Savory Spinach and Feta Pancakes

Ingredients:
1 cup all-purpose flour
1 tsp baking powder
1/2 tsp baking soda
1/4 tsp salt
1 cup milk
1 large egg
1 cup fresh spinach, chopped
1/2 cup feta cheese, crumbled

Instructions:
In a bowl, whisk flour, baking powder, baking soda, and salt. In another bowl, mix milk and egg. Combine wet and dry ingredients, then fold in spinach and feta. Cook on a skillet until golden, flipping once.

Strawberry Basil Pancakes

Ingredients:
1 cup all-purpose flour
2 tbsp sugar
1 tsp baking powder
1/2 tsp baking soda
1/4 tsp salt
1 cup milk
1 large egg
1/2 cup diced strawberries
1 tbsp fresh basil, chopped

Instructions:
In a bowl, whisk flour, sugar, baking powder, baking soda, and salt. In another bowl, mix milk and egg. Combine wet and dry ingredients, gently folding in strawberries and basil. Cook on a skillet until golden, flipping once.

Funfetti Pancakes

Ingredients:
1 cup all-purpose flour
2 tbsp sugar
1 tsp baking powder
1/2 tsp baking soda
1/4 tsp salt
1 cup milk
1 large egg
1/4 cup sprinkles

Instructions:
In a bowl, whisk flour, sugar, baking powder, baking soda, and salt. In another bowl, mix milk and egg. Combine wet and dry ingredients, folding in sprinkles. Cook on a skillet until golden, flipping once.

Honey Almond Pancakes

Ingredients:
1 cup all-purpose flour
2 tbsp sugar
1 tsp baking powder
1/2 tsp baking soda
1/4 tsp salt
1 cup milk
1 large egg
1/4 cup almond butter
1 tbsp honey

Instructions:
In a bowl, whisk flour, sugar, baking powder, baking soda, and salt. In another bowl, mix milk, egg, almond butter, and honey until smooth. Combine wet and dry ingredients. Cook on a skillet until golden, flipping once.

Matcha Coconut Pancakes

Ingredients:
1 cup all-purpose flour
2 tbsp sugar
1 tsp baking powder
1/2 tsp baking soda
1/4 tsp salt
1 cup coconut milk
1 large egg
1 tbsp matcha powder

Instructions:
In a bowl, whisk flour, sugar, baking powder, baking soda, salt, and matcha. In another bowl, mix coconut milk and egg. Combine wet and dry ingredients until just mixed. Cook on a skillet until golden, flipping once.

Enjoy these unique pancake recipes!

Chocolate Peanut Butter Pancakes

Ingredients:
1 cup all-purpose flour
2 tbsp cocoa powder
1 tbsp sugar
1 tsp baking powder
1/2 tsp baking soda
1/4 tsp salt
1 cup milk
1 large egg
1/4 cup peanut butter

Instructions:
In a bowl, whisk flour, cocoa powder, sugar, baking powder, baking soda, and salt. In another bowl, mix milk, egg, and peanut butter until smooth. Combine wet and dry ingredients until just mixed. Cook on a skillet until golden, flipping once.

Maple Bacon Pancakes

Ingredients:
1 cup all-purpose flour
2 tbsp sugar
1 tsp baking powder
1/2 tsp baking soda
1/4 tsp salt
1 cup milk
1 large egg
1/2 cup cooked bacon, chopped
1/4 cup maple syrup

Instructions:
In a bowl, whisk flour, sugar, baking powder, baking soda, and salt. In another bowl, mix milk, egg, and maple syrup. Combine wet and dry ingredients, folding in bacon. Cook on a skillet until golden, flipping once.

Muesli Pancakes

Ingredients:
1 cup all-purpose flour
1/2 cup muesli
2 tbsp sugar
1 tsp baking powder
1/2 tsp baking soda
1/4 tsp salt
1 cup milk
1 large egg

Instructions:
In a bowl, whisk flour, muesli, sugar, baking powder, baking soda, and salt. In another bowl, mix milk and egg. Combine wet and dry ingredients until just mixed. Cook on a skillet until golden, flipping once.

Raspberry Coconut Pancakes

Ingredients:
1 cup all-purpose flour
2 tbsp sugar
1 tsp baking powder
1/2 tsp baking soda
1/4 tsp salt
1 cup coconut milk
1 large egg
1/2 cup raspberries
1/4 cup shredded coconut

Instructions:
In a bowl, whisk flour, sugar, baking powder, baking soda, and salt. In another bowl, mix coconut milk and egg. Combine wet and dry ingredients, gently folding in raspberries and coconut. Cook on a skillet until golden, flipping once.

Pistachio Pancakes

Ingredients:
1 cup all-purpose flour
2 tbsp sugar
1 tsp baking powder
1/2 tsp baking soda
1/4 tsp salt
1 cup milk
1 large egg
1/4 cup crushed pistachios

Instructions:
In a bowl, whisk flour, sugar, baking powder, baking soda, and salt. In another bowl, mix milk and egg. Combine wet and dry ingredients, folding in crushed pistachios. Cook on a skillet until golden, flipping once.

Enjoy these delicious pancake recipes!

Thai Coconut Pancakes

Ingredients:
1 cup all-purpose flour
2 tbsp sugar
1 tsp baking powder
1/2 tsp baking soda
1/4 tsp salt
1 cup coconut milk
1 large egg
1/4 cup shredded coconut
1 tsp vanilla extract

Instructions:
In a bowl, whisk flour, sugar, baking powder, baking soda, and salt. In another bowl, mix coconut milk, egg, shredded coconut, and vanilla. Combine wet and dry ingredients until just mixed. Cook on a skillet until golden, flipping once.

Pear Ginger Pancakes

Ingredients:
1 cup all-purpose flour
2 tbsp sugar
1 tsp baking powder
1/2 tsp baking soda
1/4 tsp salt
1 cup milk
1 large egg
1 ripe pear, grated
1 tsp ground ginger

Instructions:
In a bowl, whisk flour, sugar, baking powder, baking soda, salt, and ginger. In another bowl, mix milk, egg, and grated pear. Combine wet and dry ingredients until just mixed. Cook on a skillet until golden, flipping once.

Tofu Pancakes

Ingredients:
1 cup all-purpose flour
1 tbsp sugar
1 tsp baking powder
1/2 tsp baking soda
1/4 tsp salt
1 cup silken tofu, blended
1/2 cup milk
1 large egg

Instructions:
In a bowl, whisk flour, sugar, baking powder, baking soda, and salt. In another bowl, blend tofu and mix with milk and egg. Combine wet and dry ingredients until just mixed. Cook on a skillet until golden, flipping once.

Cherry Almond Pancakes

Ingredients:
1 cup all-purpose flour
2 tbsp sugar
1 tsp baking powder
1/2 tsp baking soda
1/4 tsp salt
1 cup milk
1 large egg
1/2 cup cherries, pitted and chopped
1/4 cup almond slices

Instructions:
In a bowl, whisk flour, sugar, baking powder, baking soda, and salt. In another bowl, mix milk and egg. Combine wet and dry ingredients, gently folding in cherries and almond slices. Cook on a skillet until golden, flipping once.

Mocha Pancakes

Ingredients:
1 cup all-purpose flour
2 tbsp cocoa powder
1 tbsp sugar
1 tsp baking powder
1/2 tsp baking soda
1/4 tsp salt
1 cup milk
1 large egg
2 tbsp brewed coffee

Instructions:
In a bowl, whisk flour, cocoa powder, sugar, baking powder, baking soda, and salt. In another bowl, mix milk, egg, and coffee. Combine wet and dry ingredients until just mixed. Cook on a skillet until golden, flipping once.

Enjoy these delightful pancake recipes!

www.ingramcontent.com/pod-product-compliance
Lightning Source LLC
LaVergne TN
LVHW081331060526
838201LV00055B/2583